Death Rattle

Poems By
April Bulmer

ISBN 978-1-55483-596-6 (trpb)
ISBN 978-1-55483-597-3 (ebook)

Introduction

"Death Rattle" is a chapbook that tells the story of an early couple who are challenged by a plague. They respond to this sickness through pagan practices. The woman is a healer who employs unique methods to rid her family members, including her husband, of symptoms of the infectious disease that threatens their community. While her belief systems and ethnicity are not specifically named, her rituals are rooted in her own body and in the healthy powers of nature. They also reflect her deep faith in a deity called the Great Mother. Her devotion was inspired by April Bulmer's old soul. Profoundly feminine, it speaks to her of having lived as an Indigenous teacher and prehistoric cave dweller. She also recalls religious lives as a medieval Christian and as a Jewish mother.

Themes of love and sexuality are also developed throughout the short text. They are integral to the woman's response to the threat of the epidemic. The plague is a demon against whom she wages war. "Death Rattle" resonates with a haunting hack and the woman's fight to suppress it.

Author April Bulmer dedicates these poems to all First Nation people who have been wounded and committed crimes as a result. It is April's hope that she buoyed the spirits of the Indigenous men she taught in a small Canadian jail. April's heart bled at the sight of these broken men. She delivered sweetgrass so they might smudge. It brought April visions — powerful animals who walk with her still. She also dreams of the prisoners: they shine like apples in autumn. This book, however, is a fictional interpretation of pagan practices and does not reflect the true religions of First Nation men or women.

1.

I massage the moon:
her skin, marrow and bones
and apply a poultice
to her infected chest.
I speak wild horse
and mourning dove
and open the husked lips
of corncobs.
I light shadows,
offer blessings
in mother tongue.
My breasts, too,
are a source of medicine.

2.

My man dreams of my breasts
taut as apples.
My womb is an apple too.
I am fragrant with fruit.
I am clothed in weather.
In the moments before Husband wakes:
August, the dew.
I am naked and damp.
I make offerings to the ailing moon.

3.

My man and I dry ourselves
in the mourning sun.
And our clothes smell
like autumn.
"Soon the day will limp
through the dust," I say.
"Like a wounded hound.
Ghosts will hide
in the sumac trees."

4.

My man's cadence, its fall and rise
as the moon drags her sick belly
and the sun sharpens his knife.
Husband pulls his hips
against me.
He rocks to-and-fro
like a narrow boat
and my skirt floats like a flower.
When the midwife delivers our daughter,
my milk flows like a river.

5.

Demons of plague hum.
"Bring offerings," they threaten.
"Or the harvest will come."

6.

I refuse to worship demons.

I worry I am without guide.
Who courts me at night
in the pool of my mind?
Perhaps it is tortoise.
He offers a protective home, a shell.

No, it is fish who swims
into the pond of my heart.
It is resilient and quick.

I wear bear claw too.
Bear came to me in dream:
a trout dripped from the beast's
great mouth.

I hang icons from my neck.
Charms to empower and protect.

7.

My people are ill.
They speak death rattle.

My man and I kneel.
We are parishioners in the rain.
We are people of weather.

Our daughter clears her throat.
She is chilled to the bone.

The earth is sick too.
We offer her medicine.
For her tongue is thick
and her mouth infected.

8.

I mend the hem
of our old religion:
its ripped cloth and loose threads.
Still, I shiver
and mourn the dead.

I wash women
and pack moss
between their legs.
Men bury blood and rags
and bodies of folk.
I commune with ghosts.

My people plant the seeds of sorrow.
They will grow wide branches
like the maple.

9.

My drawing of an angel balanced on a rock.
I place it beside my olive-green portrait
of the Great Mother stirring in summer.
It blesses my daughter.

I create artwork for my sister, inspire her to hea
   A skull above the hearth.
   A small leaf softening to anoint.
   Our late father, a shaman, praying in a boat.

10.

My daughter still coughs
and her lungs stain the earth,
a kind of sap
on the lean belly of the land.
I am her mother.
I bore her:
birth-blood like berries.
When I lift my girl
the scent of milk on my curls.

11.

The Great Mother is history.
Her mouth is a red flower,
a bowl of rain.
Midwife and nurse, doctor.
I call her names over and over
in the shadows.
I bring offerings:
baskets of harvest pears.
Their cores are living prayers.

12.

We love the root of children.
We speak our daughter's name
to the wind
and to the night sky.
We rejoice in her healing.

13.

My man is sick.
His body is a weight
against the thin skin of the prairie.
He rests upon her.
The lines of his palms
are scars of rain
I read and predict.
I kneel before him.
Demons rise like troubled breath
from his ribs.
I kiss my man:
anoint his swollen lips.
He gasps and lives.

14.

I am ill.
The demon of plague
blows me out
like an egg.
He takes my soul then.
It is an old thing.
It bears the weight
of storms and wars
and the death
of my sister's children.
I watch him buckle
with its sorrow.
I do not suffer now.
He casts out my heart.
I am only a hollow chest.
The wind blows through
my empty breasts.

15.

My body and its curly hair
will burn.
Husband mourns.
He prays my heart
is a pod in weather.

16.

My man scatters my ashes
in a field of grazing horses.
Boys shake rattles.
They are filled with dried beans.
Girls link hands and sing.
They perform sacred dances.
Their skirts turn like autumn leaves.
Their songs touch the earth
then rise on the wind –
like me.

17.

I live in a spiritual hospital.
I am recovering still.
Angels bring me broth
and cups of medicine.
Demons cough and die.
Custodians sweep the corpses.
They are stiff and pale.
I close my third eye.

18.

I am dead
but I recall my blossoms of blood
(the dampness of woman
on her moons).
The body and its prison of bone.

19.

My man and girl embrace my spirit
during a ritual of love.
I return briefly from beyond
in a narrow boat.
A fish blesses my trip.
I am strong:
a bear tooth hangs from my throat.
My lungs have healed.
They are quiet as ghosts.

Credits

The cover image was purchased from Shutterstock.com. It is called A Rustic Scene with Rotting Apples Scattered on the Ground Near an Old, Weathered Building with a Faded Blue Door. It was photographed by Gebe Alpar.

The back-cover image was purchased from Shutterstock.com. It is called Fresh Red and Yellow Apples in Form of Heart on Green Grass. It was photographed by Leka Sergeeva.

The title-page image was purchased from Shutterstock.com. It is called Stylish Beautiful Brunette Girl in Ethnic Clothes in the Amazing Woods with Apple. It was photographed by Bogdan Sonjachnyj.

Biography

April Bulmer is a Canadian writer. She holds Master's degrees in creative writing, religion and theological studies. Central to her Honours B.A. in mass communications were courses in ballet, reggae and art history. April then studied Indigenous rituals at a Native center and ran a healing circle for First Nations incarcerated men at a jail. She travelled to Saskatchewan to commune with the voice of the prairie landscape. Some of her writing now deals with pagan spirituality and the divine feminine. While other collections focus on Christ. Many of her books have been shortlisted for awards, including the International Beverly Prize for Literature, the Pat Lowther Memorial Award, the Next Generation Indie Book Awards and the Global Book Awards. She won the YWCA Women of Distinction Award in the art and culture category in Cambridge, Ontario, where she cares for her mother. Her work has also been celebrated and published widely.

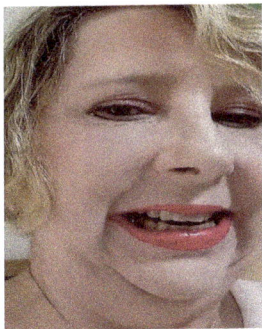

For further information about April, please
see:
www.aprilbulmer.com and
www.aprilbulmer.wordpress.com.

www.ingramcontent.com/pod-product-compliance
Lightning Source LLC
LaVergne TN
LVHW010310070426
835511LV00021B/3465